Ancient Roots of the LGBTQ
MOVEMENT

KADE
YOUNG

Contents

The Ancient Spirit

I t's so easy to get distracted by drag queen story hour in our schools and the PRIDE displays at the store. These are legitimate issues, but symptoms of the main issue.

If we can cut this thing off at the root, all the symptoms will fade away. But if we focus on the symptoms, we'll fight hard with no real resolve. So, let's get our focus on the right place.

Sodom and Gomorrah

What we are dealing with is nothing new. These issues have been around forever. We have ancient records of cultures having a sexual identity crisis. One of the most familiar is Sodom and Gomorrah.

Four thousand years ago, a man named Lot was visited by two angels. He invited them into his home. While they were there, look at what happened:

> But before they retired for the night, all the
> men of Sodom, young and old, came from all

over the city and surrounded the house. They shouted to Lot, "Where are the men who came to spend the night with you? Bring them out to us so we can have sex with them!"

Genesis 19:4-5 NLT

This city was so messed up that ALL the men in the city demanded to have sex with what they thought were the two new men in town when, in fact, they were angels.

Lot tried to protect the angels by offering his two virgin daughters in their place. (Again, this place was messed up.) But they didn't want the daughters; they wanted the men.

At this point, the angels blinded the men so that none of them could find their way inside. They finally gave up and left. God then totally destroyed Sodom and Gomorrah because the sin there became so extreme.

This was over four thousand years ago! But the same problems have resurfaced several times throughout history.

Goddess Ishtar

About 2,400 years ago, we have records of a goddess named Ishtar. Most people know her as the goddess of love, fertility, and sex. But she is also the goddess of war.

How could one goddess be known for both love and war? That's our first indicator that this is really a spirit that causes confusion. One that occupies both ends of the spectrum.

On ancient Mesopotamian tablets, the goddess described herself as follows: "When I sit in the alehouse, I am a woman, and I am an exuberant young man."[1]

In other words, Ishtar was a woman and, simultaneously, a man. She could go back and forth and express the characteristics of either gender.

You'll also find an ancient Sumerian hymn that says, "...t urn a man into a woman and a woman into a man, to change one into the other..."[2]

This goddess had male priests who presented themselves as women. They wore women's clothing, put on makeup, and paraded themselves around. Sound familiar?

There was one month out of the year when this goddess especially possessed culture. Want to guess what it was? June. And she was even known as the *goddess of pride*.

This same problem has resurfaced time and time again, each time under a new name and disguise. What once was referred to as Ishtar is now referred to as LGBTQ.

2

Infiltrating America

This war cannot be won if we are fighting a distraction. We are not fighting people. We are fighting against an ancient demonic spirit that has been allowed to infiltrate our culture.

There was a time when the LGBTQ issue was not common in America. It was around but extremely rare and kept in the shadows. America was a culture that had been cleansed of this demon.

But take a look at what happens when we drop the ball:

> When an evil spirit leaves a person, it goes into the desert, seeking rest but finding none. Then it says, 'I will return to the person I came from.' So it returns and finds its former home empty, swept, and in order. Then the spirit finds seven other spirits more evil than itself, and they all enter the person and live there. And so that person is worse off than before. That will be the

experience of this evil generation.

Matthew 12:43-45 NLT

Notice that for the demons to return, the house must be empty.

America was once full of God. The Bible was required reading in school. Every day started with prayer. Church was prioritized over everything else, even kids' sports.

But then, in 1962, prayer was taken out of schools. A few years later, the feminist movement took off. Soon after, in 1973, it became legal to murder children in the womb.

This house we call America was once full of God. But when we took God out, it gave place for these ancient evil spirits to come in and possess an entire generation.

How It Possessed America

This ancient spirit has three main strategies. First, it alters the definition of male and female. Then, it works to feminize males and masculinize females. Finally, it has completed its goal of blurring the lines of sexuality and gender.

How does this spirit manifest in women?

They develop a disdain for male leadership. They buy into the feminism movement—or maybe I should say "women's rights"—and gloat about their independence, saying, "I don't need a man. I can do it myself." They covet a man's job.

How does it manifest in men?

They act like overgrown children living in their mom's basement. They are unfit for leadership. They are weak and pitiful, walking around with a victim mentality. They become consumed with appearance.

From Feminism to LGBTQ

Make no mistake. What started as feminism has become LGBTQ and every sexual perversion you see today.

Feminism was the bait offered by this ancient demonic spirit. A majority of women took it hook, line, and sinker. This evil spirit used these women to accomplish the end goal.

Now, feminism has been destroyed by transgenderism. What was supposedly "women's rights" was really a war on women. Our culture doesn't even know what a woman is anymore.

Altering the God-assigned role of males and females is how it all started. For the enemy to get the foothold he has now gained, he had to blur the lines and disguise it as *equality*.

Once the foundation was laid, this ancient demonic spirit could unleash the sexual and gender identity crises going on today.

The Real Enemy

Can you see who the real enemy is? Here's how Ephesians explains it:

For we are not fighting against flesh-and-blood enemies, but against evil rulers and authorities of the unseen world, against mighty powers in this dark world, and against evil spirits in the heavenly places.

Ephesians 6:12 NLT

We are at war with evil spirits. Don't get distracted by what you see. Keep your focus on the real issue so we can cut it off at the root.

A massive move of deliverance is coming for those being tormented by these evil spirits. As soon as we realize it's a spiritual issue, we can exercise our authority in Christ to cast out evil spirits and free the captives.

Demon Possession Explained

Now that we know the problem, how do we eliminate it? Let's turn to Jesus for the answer.

Once when he [Jesus] was in the synagogue, a man **possessed** by a demon—an evil spirit—cried out, shouting, "Go away! Why are you interfering with us, Jesus of Nazareth? Have you come to destroy us? I know who you are—the Holy One of God!" But Jesus reprimanded him. "Be quiet! Come out of the man," he ordered. At that, the demon threw the man to the floor as the crowd watched; then it came out of him without hurting him further. Amazed, the people exclaimed, "What authority and power this man's words possess! Even evil spirits obey him, and they flee at his command!"

Luke 4:33-36 NLT

The New Living Translation uses the word *possess*. And that's how most of us would think about a situation like this. We would call them *possessed*.

But take a look at what the New King James Version says:

> Now in the synagogue there was a man who **had** a spirit of an unclean demon.

What does this word translated to *had* in the NKJV and *possess* in NLT actually mean?

In the original Greek language, the word is "echo," and it means:

- To hold in the hand; to wear

- To have possession of the mind

- To be joined together[3]

Notice it says nothing about having possession of your spirit. Yet that is how most of us think about demonic issues. We think it's a full-on possession, spirit, soul, and body.

This line of thinking gives the devil too much credit. I've yet to find where the Bible says a demon can possess a person's spirit.

Your body? Yes. Your mind? Yes. And digging into this Greek word *echo* gives us insight into how this happens.

THE PROGRESSION

Demonic issues don't happen overnight. There is a normal progression.

It all starts when someone begins to hold on to the things of the devil, putting them on and wearing them like clothing. We're talking about any kind of sin that you embrace. As you continue to *wear* these things, the devil takes possession of your mind.

At this point, you can't stop thinking about that sin. Your thoughts drive you deeper and deeper into darkness.

As the thoughts progress, soon you become *joined together* with this thing, much like a marriage. No longer can you just casually walk away from it. Now you have to get a full-on *divorce*.

That's why the demon threw the man on the ground on its way out in the previously mentioned scripture. Divorce is not pretty.

How the LGBTQ Spirit
Takes Root

I f you read my book, *Jesus Ain't Woke*, you know that I was delivered from homosexuality. This progression outlined in the previous chapter matches exactly what I went through.

It started with me picking it up and putting it back down. Picking it up again and putting it back down. Then I picked it up and put it on, wearing it like an article of clothing. It didn't take long before it possessed my mind.

At that point, I became joined together with this unclean spirit. I had a demon. But only because I opened the door and allowed it in.

This will throw you for a loop. I grew up in church. My grandpa was a pastor. We were in church every Sunday and every Wednesday. I loved God. I loved the church. I loved Jesus.

I was even leading a youth worship band. God's presence would fill the room in the midst of the worship services I was leading. Yet, I was joined together with an unclean spirit. I had a demon.

Did I feel conflicted inside? Oh, yeah. I should have been diagnosed as bipolar because I was one person at church and another at school. Almost daily, I would be thrilled by the unclean spirit, and then be crying out for God's forgiveness that night.

No one knew I was being tormented. When I was at church, I was all in. When I was with the wrong crowd, I was all in. Those on both sides of my life thought I was good. But I wasn't.

I thought it was just me. I was fighting myself. I was asking God for forgiveness. I was making promises that I would never do it again. But nothing was working.

Add to all this, various people were telling me, "Why are you fighting this? It's how you were born. It's nothing to be ashamed of."

Speaking of which, let's pause for a moment while I counter that lie right now.

BORN GAY?

There is no proof that homosexuality is a genetic disposition that cannot be escaped. Even Harvard did a study and could not prove people are born gay.[4]

It's well known in the scientific community that if homosexuality were genetic, then if one identical twin were homosexual, 100% of the time, the other would be too. But that's not the case.

So, there's nothing to prove that people are born gay. But there are plenty of people who can prove otherwise.

No one is born gay. Homosexuality is a demonic stronghold from which people can be delivered. Jesus gives every believer the power to live in freedom.

Other Demonic Causes

A lthough the previous two chapters revealed one of the most common causes of demonic issues, there are others that need to be examined. This scripture provides more insight into how demons torment people.

> When they came down from the mountain, the disciples stood with Jesus on a large, level area, surrounded by many of his followers and by the crowds. There were people from all over Judea and from Jerusalem and from as far north as the seacoasts of Tyre and Sidon. They had come to hear him and to be healed of their diseases; and those **troubled** by evil spirits were healed. Everyone tried to touch him, because healing power went out from him, and he healed everyone.
> **Luke 6:17-19 NLT**

In Luke 4, Jesus delivered a man who HAD a demon. This scripture says He delivered those TROUBLED by demons. Let's dig into the word translated to 'troubled' so we can understand the difference.

- To excite a mob against one

- To harass, disturb, trouble

- To be molested by demons[5]

Wow. That last definition brings a lot of clarity. Some people with demons were molested by demons at a young age or at a weak point in their lives. There's a study that proves this. The study found that sexually abused young males are up to 70% more likely to self-identify as gay than their peers who were not abused.[6]

Many of those who struggle with their sexual identity do so because of something that happened when they were young. They may have been introduced to pornography at a young age. Or, they may have even been sexually abused by someone of the same sex. Whatever the case, they were essentially molested and tormented by the demonic realm.

Out of Hiding

Now we know that people can have demons because they opened the door by engaging in sin or demonic things. Others have demons because they were molested by demons.

There are even those who had a mob of demons sent against them. And, because they didn't know their authority in Christ, they continue to deal with those demons today.

Whatever the cause, in order to receive deliverance, you must first recognize you need it. That demon has to come out of hiding so it can be cast out.

Exposing Evil Spirits

In Luke, chapter four, the man with an unclean spirit came to church that day and sat quietly, listening to Jesus teach.

We don't know for sure, but I bet he went to church that day in search of a way out of his torment. He'd heard about the amazing teaching of Jesus and probably thought, "He has the answer."

The teaching of Jesus was so agitating to the demon that it cried out. It couldn't hide any longer. It knew its time was limited. With a **simple command**, Jesus delivered this man from his torment. He made the demon leave, but he let the man stay.

These days, when there is a manifestation like this at church, many church leaders would leave the demon in the person, but ask the person to leave. Let me remind you of what Jesus actually told us to do regarding this:

And these signs will follow those who believe:

In My name they will cast out demons...

Mark 16:17 NKJV

An automatic sign of following Jesus is casting out demons. There are others as well, but the first on the list is casting out demons. If it's the first on the list, that means it will be a frequent occurrence. So, what's going on?

WHERE ARE THE DEMONS?

I've been in church for 35 years. I was a worship leader for ten years. I've been a lead pastor for five years. But it wasn't until recently that I began to witness demons being cast out of people.

Does that mean there were no demons around here all this time? Or have we become so accustomed to them that we let them hang around?

All a person has to do is look at the state of our nation to know that demons are definitely having a heyday in America. That means it must be the latter. We have become desensitized to unclean spirits.

They do their best to fly under the radar. Demons do not want to be noticed. But why have we been allowing them to do so?

Why don't we do what Jesus did and agitate them so much that they must manifest? This is an important part of deliverance because if we don't know it's there, how can we cast it out?

Unhindered Word of God

The bold teaching of Jesus agitated that demon so much that it came out of hiding and manifested itself. So that's the first step. Agitate the demons with the unhindered Word of God.

You can't water it down. You can't skirt around unpopular issues like homosexuality. The only way to agitate the demonic realm is with the unhindered Word of God. It must come out of your mouth like a sword.

But you can't just stop there. Once the demon makes itself known, you have to cast it out.

Casting Out Demons

Once a demon is exposed, it must be cast out. Most Christians would get scared at this point, as if the demon has more power than they do. Most church leaders would try to "protect the church's reputation" by removing the person.

Jesus told us to do neither of those. He didn't say to run and hide. He didn't say to keep things nice and calm. He said to cast out demons. It should be a regular occurrence.

DEMONS HANGING AROUND

So why are we letting demons hang around? Because we've been duped. Casting out demons is too messy. It doesn't fit into our perfect-performance church services.

It doesn't work with the seeker-sensitive church model, where we are urged to create church services that make lost people comfortable.

Nothing about following Jesus was promised to be comfortable! He never told us to make people comfortable. Actually, He made it very clear that following Him is uncomfortable. You have to crucify your flesh daily!

On top of all this comfort nonsense, we've been taught that a Christian cannot have a demon. So people are going to church every Sunday while living in a constant state of torment.

We tell them to read the Bible more. We tell them to go see the doctor and get meds. We tell them to go through a 12-step program.

At the risk of making enemies, I still have to make this known. If a demon is causing the torment, the only way to get rid of it is to cast it out. Medicine won't work. Prayer won't work. Memorizing scripture won't work. Not for this!

We must stop devising our own solutions and do what Jesus told us to do: cast the demons out!

Am I saying that *everything* is a demon? No. But on the other hand, we can't keep acting like *nothing* is a demon.

Just look at the ministry of Jesus. One of the first things He did was cast out a demon. Then He kept at it, casting out demons everywhere He went. Then He had His disciples cast out demons. Then He told us to cast out demons.

This tells me that there are demons to be cast out. And they are not just tormenting non-believers. They are tormenting people right within the church.

CHRISTIANS AND DEMONS

Even as a born-again believer, you can pick up sin and put it back down. You can pick it up and put it on. You can keep it around so that it consumes your mind and then joins together with you.

That was me. I was joined together with that unclean spirit of homosexuality. Until one day, I'd had enough.

I was in my bedroom seeking God when I dropped to my knees and said, "God, I don't just want your forgiveness. I want freedom. Take this thing from me so I can live for you."

At that moment, I sensed something leave my body. And in its place, I was overwhelmed with the love of God. I was weeping uncontrollably because I knew I was finally free.

Deliverance happens in a moment.

After this, I was no longer consumed with homosexuality. It still presented itself as a temptation, but now I had the power to overcome it.

I am overjoyed to report that I haven't picked up that sin since the day I was delivered. Not only that, but I'm enjoying a 16-year marriage with my beautiful wife, and God has given us five precious children!

Now, if Satan presents his temptation, it's quite humorous. First of all, I am no longer a slave to sin. God provides a way out of every temptation. Plus, why would I risk my family to engage in something set to destroy me? Satan is a loser.

READY FOR FREEDOM?

Do you need freedom? Make a decision right now to cut ties with that unclean spirit so it can be cast out. Because if you want to keep it, God will not override your will. It's up to you.

If a demon can convince you that this is not a demonic issue, you'll stay in bondage. You'll stay tormented in your mind. Because if the cause is a demon, nothing will work except casting it out.

If you are afraid that it will come out screaming, throw you on the ground, and ruin your reputation, that demon is perfectly fine hiding behind your pride. But as soon as you find out the torment in your life is caused by a demon and you decide to cut ties with it no matter how ugly the divorce is, freedom is yours, my friend.

This all sounds terrifying, but it's really not. Expose the demon, surrender to Jesus Christ, and use His authority to command the demons to come out.

So go ahead. The time for freedom is NOW. You can have someone who believes in casting out demons join you, or you can get alone with Jesus and get it taken care of. Once you expose the demon and surrender to Jesus, you'll be shocked at how easy it is to get rid of that unclean spirit.

Maintaining Freedom

O nce you are free, you must know your authority in Christ so you don't open yourself back up to the same torment. You can also use the same authority to help others find freedom. That's why I am wrapping up this book with a brief explanation of the authority of Christ.

ALL AUTHORITY

After Jesus rose from the dead, He had a few things to tell the disciples before He ascended into heaven. Here is one of them:

> Jesus came and told his disciples, "I have been given all authority in heaven and on earth."
> **Matthew 28:18 NLT**

How much authority? **All.** Jesus is the King of Kings.

Where does the authority work? **In heaven and on earth.** Jesus has all authority in the spiritual realm and the physical realm.

Can you see why the modern representation of Jesus as this super nice guy who tolerates everything is so dangerous? That's a counterfeit Jesus. People are believing in a fake Jesus and will end up in hell if they don't meet the real Jesus.

The real Jesus is a boss. God has given Him all authority in heaven and on earth. His power is unmatched. All things are under His jurisdiction.

If you picture Him as the tolerant Jesus, you cannot live under His authority. Don't buy into a hippy Jesus. That's not who He is. He is the King of Kings. His strength is endless. His power is unmatched.

SUBMISSION REQUIRED

I hope you can now see Jesus as He really is. Yes, He is your savior. But in order to spend eternity with Him, He has to be more than just your savior. He has to be your Lord. Let me put it to you this way:

There will be no one in heaven who refuses to submit to the authority of Christ.

Salvation requires you to confess Jesus Christ as Lord. You must bow to the King of kings.

CAN YOU BE SAVED AND GAY?

This brings up a common question. Can you be saved and gay? Even those who have never struggled with homosexuality probably know someone who has. So this is a question almost every Christian wrestles with at some point.

The Bible says that salvation requires two things.[7] First, you must believe that God raised Jesus from the dead. Second, you must openly declare Jesus is your Lord.

When you declare Jesus as Lord, it means you have decided to abandon your desires and submit to the way of Jesus. He knows you won't get it perfect. Perfection is not required. Quick repentance is what is required. When King Jesus tells you to get something out of your life, you quickly turn away from that thing and follow Jesus.

So, can you be saved and gay? Maybe for a little while. But it doesn't take long to figure out that homosexuality is not the way of Christ. And since Jesus is Lord, you leave that lifestyle as you submit to Christ.

If you don't abandon homosexuality, you reveal that Jesus isn't your Lord. Instead, you are saying, "My way is better." That's why this is called the PRIDE movement because everyone who participates is saying, "My way is better. I don't care that I just destroyed my family. I don't care that God considers it an abomination. I'm going to do what I want."

But know this. When Jesus becomes not just your Savior but your Lord, when you truly submit yourself to Him, He will give you the power to live free from homosexuality. He did it for me, and He can do it for you.

And here's the best part. As soon as you submit to His authority, you *have* His authority. You don't have to be tormented by demons anymore.

USING THE AUTHORITY OF CHRIST

How do we know that we can operate under the authority of Christ?

> One day Jesus called together his twelve disciples and gave them power and authority to cast out all demons and to heal all diseases.
> **Luke 9:1-2 NLT**

Jesus gives His authority to His followers, complete with instructions on how to use it: cast out demons and heal all diseases.

Like most American Christians, I used to ignore the first part of this instruction to cast out demons. I reasoned that it was only needed in other countries. Well, I'm not going to ignore it anymore. With His authority, I will live in freedom and set the captives free, just like Jesus told me to. Will you join me?

You don't have to tolerate demons. Submit yourself to Jesus Christ and use His authority to live in freedom. Then, use that same authority to lead others to freedom in Christ. Let's cleanse our nation of these ancient evil spirits.

Let's lead people to true freedom in Jesus.

Share this book with others.

Order additional copies on Amazon

Share the video version.

Watch for free at KadeYoung.com

Cast out demons.

Made possible by Jesus Christ

About the Author
KADE YOUNG

Once a homosexual, now a free man for more than 18 years. The power of Jesus Christ set Kade free from sin and he can't help but share it with others.

He is the lead pastor of NoLimits Church. Graduate of Rhema Bible College. Husband to Beth and a blessed father of five.

Kade is the author of Jesus Ain't Woke, where he reveals the Biblical view of Critical Race Theory, abortion, LGBTQ in a thrilling 30-minute read.

He is the founder of Collaborate Worship, where he teaches hundreds of thousands of churches around the world how to make it easy to create great sound.

Kade is a newbie farmer, learning how to raise sheep, cattle, and chickens. Basically, any excuse to be outside and Kade is in—especially hiking in Colorado.

Learn more at **kadeyoung.com**

Endnotes

1. ETCSL 4.07.9, pp. 16–20

2. ETCSL 4.07.3

3. Summarized from *Thayer's Greek Lexicon*

4. https://www.harvardmagazine.com/2019/08/there-s
   -still-no-gay-gene

5. Summarized from *Thayer's Greek Lexicon*

6. https://www.ncbi.nlm.nih.gov/pmc/articles/PMC35
   35560/

7. Romans 10:9

Made in the USA
Coppell, TX
18 June 2024